A Dynasty
of Dinosaurs

ISBN: 978-1-932926-42-2

Artemesia Publishing, LLC
9 Mockingbird Hill Rd
Tijeras, New Mexico 87059
info@artemesiapublishing.com
www.apbooks.net

A Dynasty
of Dinosaurs

Illustrated by
Jason Poole

Written by
Jason P. Schein

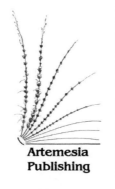

**Artemesia
Publishing**

Dedication

We dedicate this book to our children; Arielle, Izzy, Jackson and Lilly . . .
May your lives forever be colored by science and nature . . .

Special thanks to David Schloss for creating the title.

"Paleontology is the culmination of, and a perfect match for, a
life full of curiosity and love for the natural world."
    ~ Jason Poole and Jason P Schein

Introduction

As an artist, I think I may view the history of our planet with a bit of a bias. No don't stop reading! My point is this. The coolest animals in the Devonian basically looked like flying saucers with sharks up their bums, and Ice Age critters were wicked cool, but seem to hide all the cool anatomy under wooly fur. The animals of the present day are alive and totally viewable running around in their habitats, so no mystery there...

But the dinosaurs of the Mesozoic!!! That's where the fun is! From the tiny to the supermassive, carnivores or totally tricked-out herbivores, the dinosauria has it all. You want horns and frills... Dinosaurs. You want teeth and claws... Dinosaurs. Plates and spikes... need I say it... Dinosaurs.

Fossils are where we start when trying to understand the world that dinosaurs inhabited millions of years ago, and imagination helps to unlock those stories. This book is a work of fictional images based on what we know about dinosaurs and imagination. In just the few years that it took to illustrate this book, we have learned so much more about these amazing animals. Some that are pictured within we now know may have been covered in feathers. Some may have had different anatomy altogether - *Spinosaurus* is a perfect example! These changes are due to the tireless work of researchers all around the world. As this book ages, more and more things that are "known" will change; that is the nature of science. Each change then opens doors for future researchers, paleo-illustrators, and, dare I say, coloring books.

Enjoy this book, share it with friends, use lots of methods to color the images, and make them your own.

Stay tuned for more books like this one.

Rock on!

~ Jason Poole

Dinosaurs!

The terrible lizards may be the most amazing living things to ever inhabit the planet. They included the largest animals known to exist, the largest and most vicious predators ever to walk the earth, and they even became the sparrows, turkeys, and ostriches of today! There were thousands of species of dinosaurs, inhabiting every continent, for more than 160 million years. Just in the last 150 years, paleontologists have learned so much about how these remarkable creatures lived and interacted with each other and their environments. We still learn more every day, but there's still so much more to discover!

A big part of science is the process of classifying things, like plants, animals, and rocks, or organizing them into groups. Dinosaurs are no exception. Dinosaurs are divided into two main groups based on the arrangement of their hip bones. The saurischian (meaning "lizard-hip") dinosaurs include all of the therapods, or meat eaters, and the sauropods. The ornithischian ("bird-hipped) dinosaurs include all of the other herbivores. As you go through this book, you will see similarities in the body structures of many dinosaurs – see if you can figure out which ones belong in the same groups.

The Artist's Eye

Fun Fact:

Paleontologists discover a new species of dinosaur just about every 2 weeks!

The Sauropods & Prosauropods

The sauropods were an amazing group of dinosaurs that lived all over the planet. Although their ancestors – the Prosauropods, like *Plateosaurus* – were smaller and walked on two legs, the more familiar sauropods walked on four legs and are known for their long necks and even longer tails. Some of the sauropods were so heavy scientists used to think they must have lived in swamps and shallow lakes to support their weight. But no more! We now know they were right at home living on the land, eating hundreds of pounds of plants every day.

Fun Fact:

Amphicoelus is both the longest (nearly 200 feet long) and heaviest (122 tons, or 244,000 lbs!) animal ever to live on Earth!

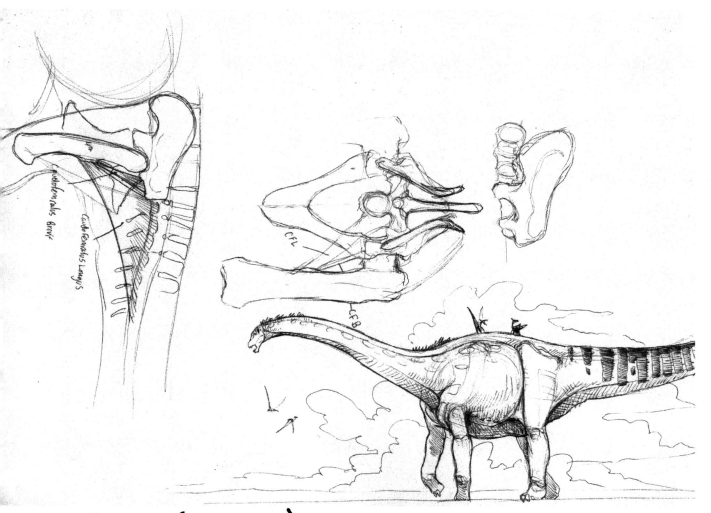

The Artist's Eye

Fun Fact:

Paleontologists aren't sure what *Amargasaurus*' neck spines were used for. Were they spines that stuck out from the next like spikes, or did they support a sail of skin?

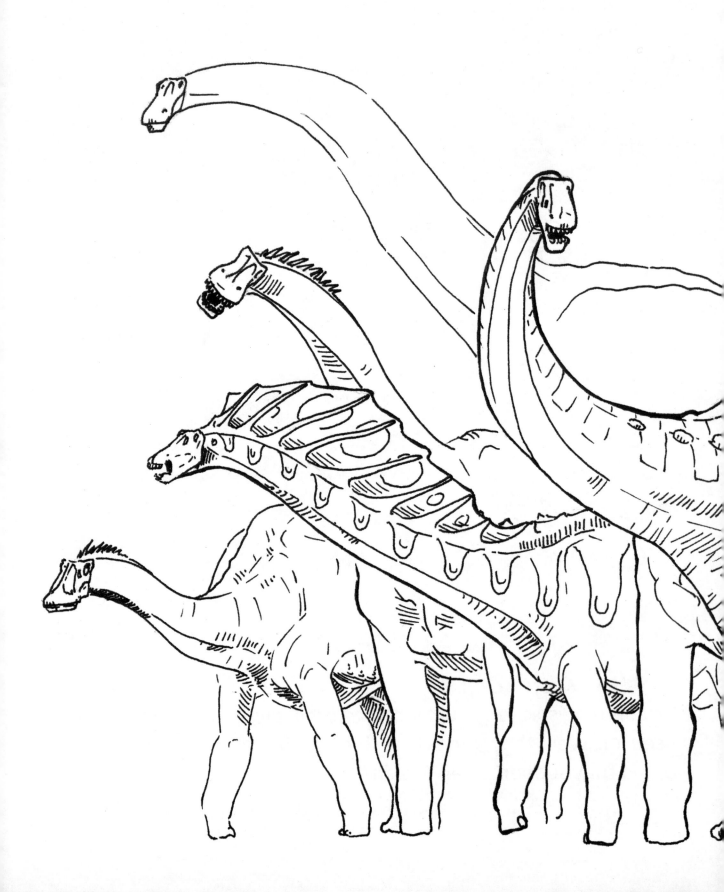

The Ceratopsians

Everyone recognizes *Triceratops*, but there is much more to the ceratopsians -or "horn-face" dinosaurs - than just that one iconic species. The ceratopsians are a diverse group of herbivores mostly from the Cretaceous Period, and their distinctive facial horns and frills come in a wide variety of sizes and arrangements. *Centrosaurus* had just one rostral (nose) horn and two smaller ones that curved and pointed down from the top of its frill. *Stryacosaurus* also had a rostral horn, as well as one protruding from each cheek, and six on its frill.

The Artist's Eye

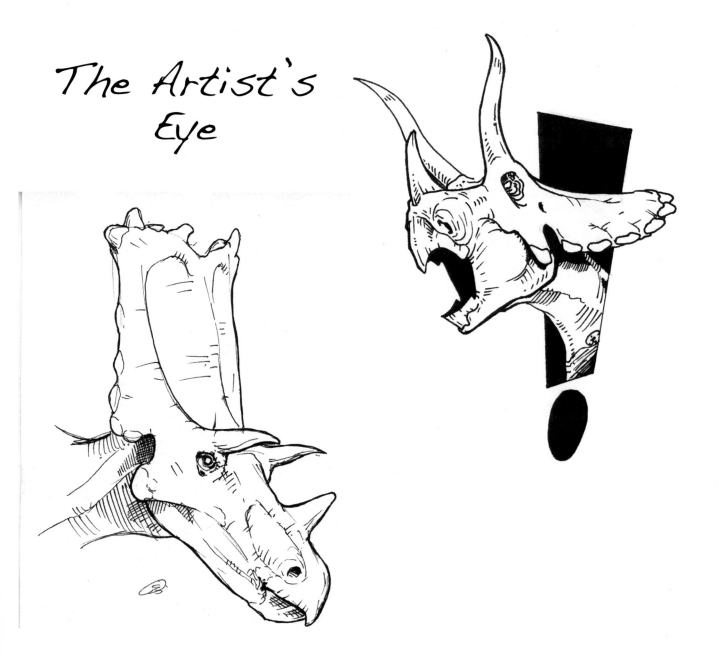

Fun Fact:

Was the famous ceratopsian neck frill used as a shield to defend itself from predators? Was it used more as a signal to attract mates, or to ward off potential rivals? The answer is probably "Yes!" It is likely that the shield was used for all of these things throughout their lives. It is also possible that it was used to help regulate body temperature.

Nigersaurus

Nigersaurus was a rather small sauropod at only 30 feet (9 m) long, and as its name suggests, was first found in Niger, Africa. This dinosaur had one of the most bizarre mouths in the animal kingdom: wide and straight, its mouth resembled a vacuum cleaner attachment. The distinctive mouth shape, along with up to 600 teeth, certainly must have helped vacuum up just about any plants nearby. We also know that its head was pointed down, which indicates that *Nigersaurus* specialized on low-growing plants.

The Artist's Eye

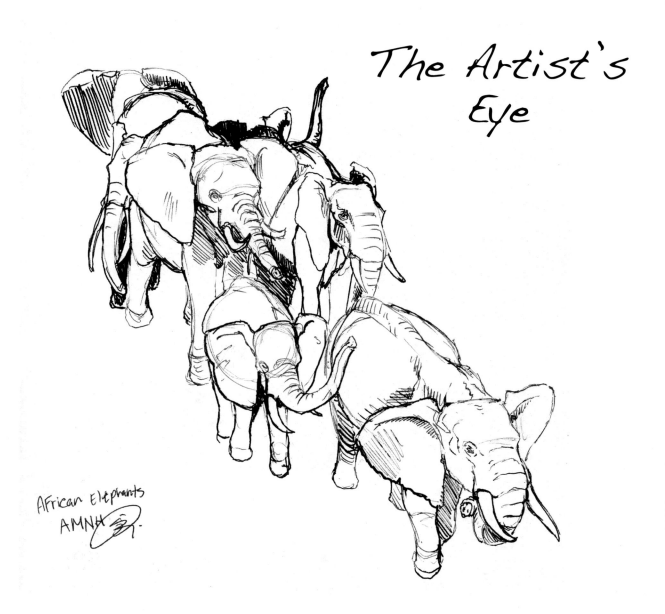

African Elephants
AMNH

Fun Fact:

Despite all of those teeth, *Nigersaurus* did not chew its food. Many of its skull bones were only millimeters thick – too thin for strong chewing muscled to have been attached.

Tyrannosaurus rex Mother and Juvenile

T. rex certainly was a ferocious predator – perhaps the largest terrestrial predator ever to walk the earth. However, they may have had a softer side as well. We know that at least some species of dinosaurs took care of their young, much like their crocodile and alligator cousins do today. We also know that many species of therapods - the group of meat-eating dinosaurs to which *T. rex* belongs - were covered in feathers. A large predator, like an adult *T. rex*, would not have needed the insulation provided by feathers, but small, young individuals may have had feathers until adulthood.

The Artist's Eye

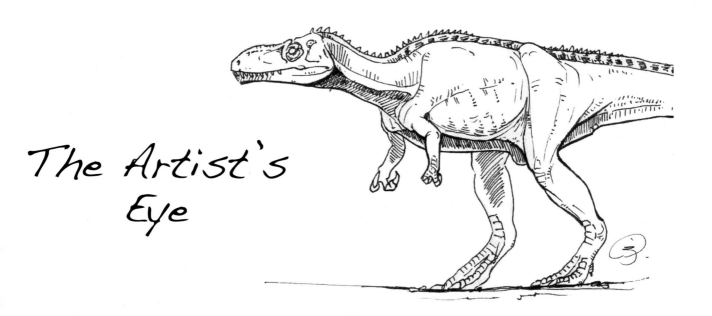

Fun Fact:

Was *Nanotyrannus* a small, close relative of *Tyrannosaurus rex*, or is it actually a juvenile *T. rex*? Paleontologists still aren't sure. The only way to know is to find more skeletons!

Therizinosaurus

Many dinosaur species had strange looking body parts, but *Therizinosaurus* may be the weirdest of all. Their general body shape, especially the large "pot" belly, was unlike almost any other species. They're also famous for their enormous hand claws. Those three foot long, samurai sword-shaped claws on each finger are the longest claws known in the animal kingdom. The most bizarre thing, though, is that *Therizinosaurus* didn't use these claws as weapons for hunting – it was an herbivore! The claws were probably used to help it collect leaves and fruit, perhaps the same way modern sloths use their claws today.

White Rhinoceros

Black Rhino

The Artist's Eye

Fun Fact:

Therozinosaurus was first discovered in 1948 in Mongolia, but it wasn't until 1970 that we had anything more than its claws. Until then, paleontologists thought those claws belonged to an enormous turtle.

Parasaurolophus

Parasaurolophus belongs to the Lambeosaurines: the crested hadrosaurs. It was quite large for a hadrosaur, reaching more than 30 feet (9 m) long and two and a half tons. Its most distinctive feature however, is the large cranial crest. For decades, paleontologists weren't sure what it was used for. Defense? Visual cue to rivals and mates? A Snorkel? Thanks to some remarkably well-preserved skulls and advances in technology, we now know that the crest was hollow, creating an effective resonance chamber, much like a musical instrument. *Parasaurolophus* used its crest for communicating with other members of the herd!

Fun Fact:

Paleontologists have used computers to analyze the cranial crest and determine what kind of sounds *Parasaurolophus* could have made. We now can hear what one of these dinosaurs sounded like more than 65 million years ago!

Ichthyosaur

Ichthyosaurs were marine reptiles that ruled the seas from the Late Triassic Period until the Early Cretaceous Period (220 – 120 million years ago) when they were replaced as the ocean's apex predator by the plesiosaurs. Although they look very much like modern dolphins, they are not at all closely related. Like dolphins, though, they were probably swift, agile predators of fish, smaller reptiles, and the ancient relatives of squid. Some species of ichthyosaurs had extremely large eyes, indicating that they may have hunted in the dark depths of the oceans.

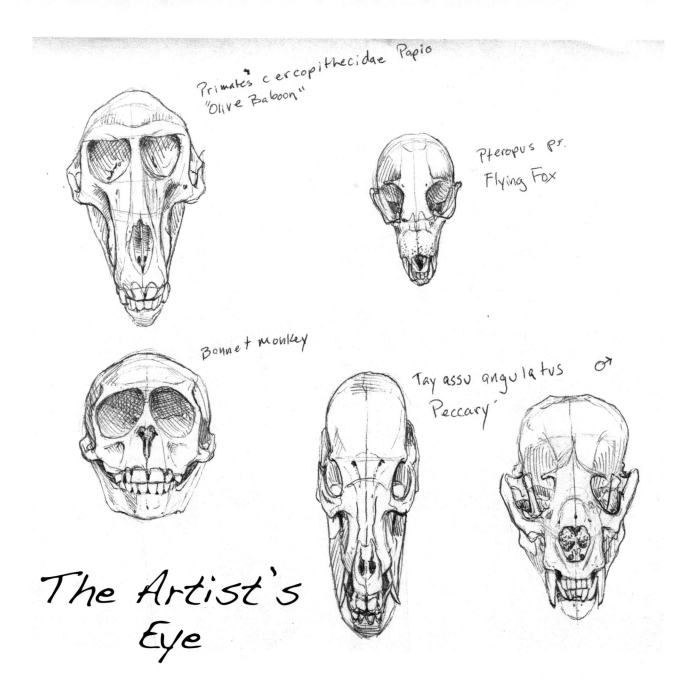

Primates cercopithecidae Papio
"Olive Baboon"

Pteropus pr.
Flying Fox

Bonnet monkey

Tayassu angulatus ♂
Peccary

The Artist's Eye

Fun Fact:
Some remarkable fossils have shown us that ichthyosaurs were warm blooded and that they gave birth to live young.

The Hadrosaurs

The hadrosaurs, or duck-billed dinosaurs, were a very diverse and successful group of ornithischians ("bird-hipped" dinosaurs) during the Cretaceous Period. With dozens of species known and more being found each year, paleontologists divide the hadrosaurs into two groups: the crested Lambeosaurines and the crestless Hadrosaurines. All of the duck-billed dinosaurs were herbivores and used hundreds of teeth to grind down tough vegetation. They were probably highly social animals that lived and migrated in great herds, and fossil evidence shows us that they were a favorite prey of larger predators, like *T. rex*.

Tethyshadros insularis
JVP   Volume 29, #4 December 2009
PG 1100

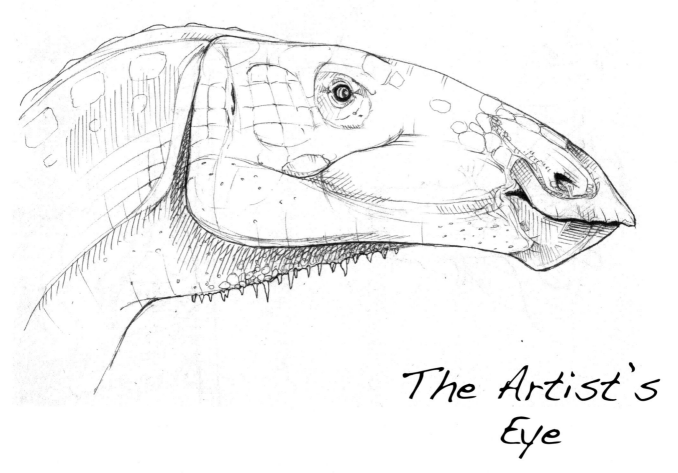

The Artist's
Eye

Fun Fact:

The first nearly complete dinosaur skeleton in the world – a hadrosaur named *Hadrosaurus foulkii* – was discovered in southern
New Jersey, U.S.A., in 1858.

Carnotaurus

Carnotaurus, which means "flesh-eating bull", was a fierce predator named for the distinctive horns over its eyes. Weighing up to 2,000 pounds and reaching 30 feet long, *Carnotaurus* must have been the apex predator of South America during the Late Cretaceous. Paleontologists aren't sure whether their massive heads and thick, muscular necks helped them to hunt large prey, like the many enormous sauropods that shared the same ecosystems, or smaller, more agile prey. They also aren't sure of the purpose for the characteristic brow horns. Were they for fighting, or used as visual cues? We need more skeletons to find out!

The Artist's Eye

Fun Fact:

We know a lot about *Carnotaurus*, but it is all based on a single, remarkably well-preserved skeleton found in Argentina. The remains even included skin impressions!

Amargasaurus

Discovered by the same team that discovered *Carnotaurus*, *Amargasaurus* may be the strangest of all of the sauropods. At just over 30 feet (9 m) long and weighing 2.5 tons, *Amargasaurus* was small for a sauopod, but its most distinctive feature is the two rows of long spines that extended along the back of its neck. Scientists aren't certain about how these spines may have looked in life. They may have been simple spines, or they may have supported a sail of skin. We also aren't certain about what they were used for: they were too thin to be useful for defense, especially with large predators like *Carnotaurus* around.

The Artist's Eye

Fun Fact:

Amargasaurus had a close relative, *Dicraeosaurus*, which also had a double row of spikes along its neck. These spikes, though, were only a few inches long.

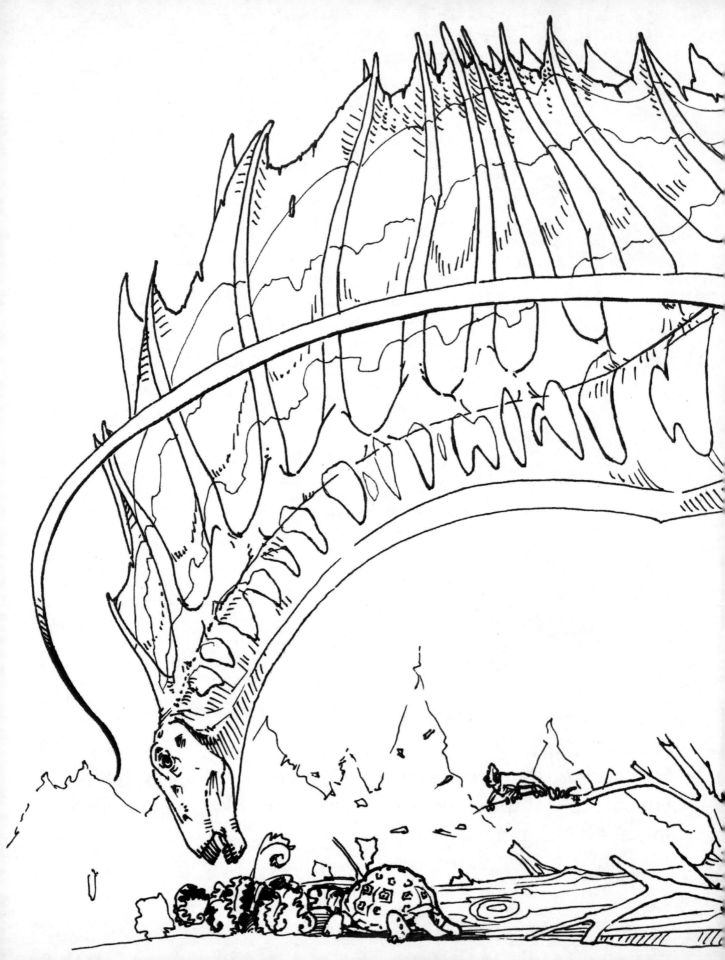

Spinosaurids

Most therapods, or meat-eating dinosaurs, had short, broad, powerful skulls and jaws, designed for crushing and tearing. Spinosaurids, however, like *Spinosaurus*, *Baryonyx*, and *Irritator*, had long, slender jaws, much like crocodiles have today. This suggests that they were specialized for capturing small prey, like fish, with rapid, powerful movements. Some paleontologists even think that they were semi-aquatic, spending much of their time in water. Even though the entire group is most often associated with a large sail on their backs, only *Spinosaurus* actually has that anatomical feature.

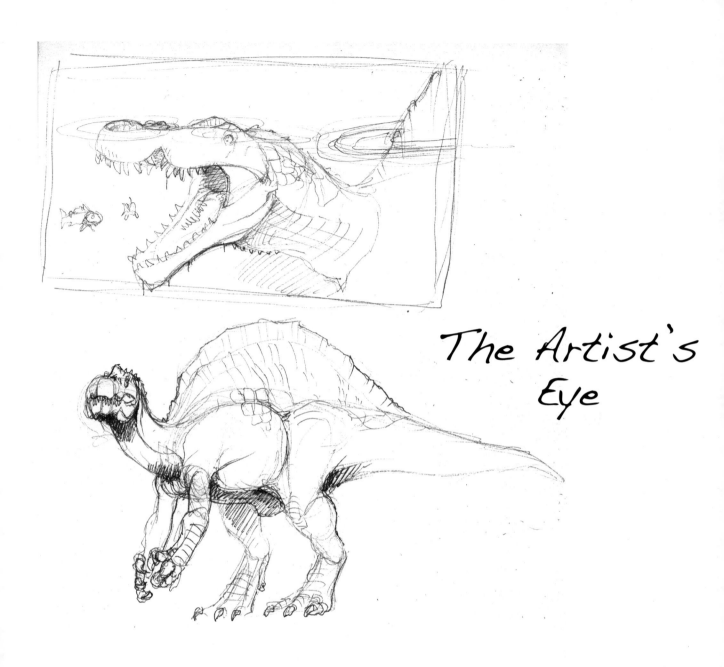

The Artist's Eye

Fun Fact:

Spinosaurus fossils are found in North Africa, but spinosaurid remains also have been found in Europe, South America, Asia, and Australia.

Spinosaurus Family

Spinosaurus lived very much like crocodiles and alligators do today – lounging in the sun beside lakeshores, or spending a lot of time in the water ambushing small prey with quick, long, slender jaws. Most paleontologists think *Spinosaurus* was piscivorous – specialized for eating fish. Thanks to a recent, remarkable discovery, we now know a lot more about this famous dinosaur. Before 2014, only one skeleton of *Spinosaurus* has even been found, and sadly, that skeleton was destroyed in Germany in World War II.

The Artist's Eye

Fun Fact:

Some scientists have interpreted the sail on *Spinosaurus'* back to actually be a fatty or muscular hump, much like a camel's hump.

Stegosaurs

The stegosaurs are a fascinating group of quadrupedal herbivores from the Jurassic and Early Cretaceous periods. They all had small, narrow heads, large bodies, and are easily recognized by the rows of osteoderms, or bones, that grow as plates and spikes along their back. They also have a tail studded with spikes, called a "thagomizer." The thagomizer was definitely an effective defensive weapon, but paleontologists are less sure of the plates' purpose. It is possible they were used for defense, for regulating body temperatures, or as a visual cue for mates and rivals. It's very likely, however, that the plates did all of those things.

ALBERTOSAURUS
AMNH

The Artist's Eye

Fun Fact:

The stegosaurs are closely related to the armored dinosaurs, like *Ankylosaurus*. Together, they form the group of dinosaurs called the Thyreophora.

Kentrosaurus

Because of their large bodies and short front legs, stegosaurs were pretty slow, which means they needed lots of protection from predators. *Kentrosaurus*, which inhabited Africa more than 150 million years ago, was certainly up to the challenge. With a double row of bony plates and long, sharp spikes running the length of its back, *Kentrosaurus* was one of the most well-armored dinosaurs known. Its huge shoulder spikes, though, are what distinguish it from other stegosaurs. Any predatory attack on *Kentrosaurus* would be risky, requiring a lot of planning, skill, and a bit of luck.

The Artist's Eye

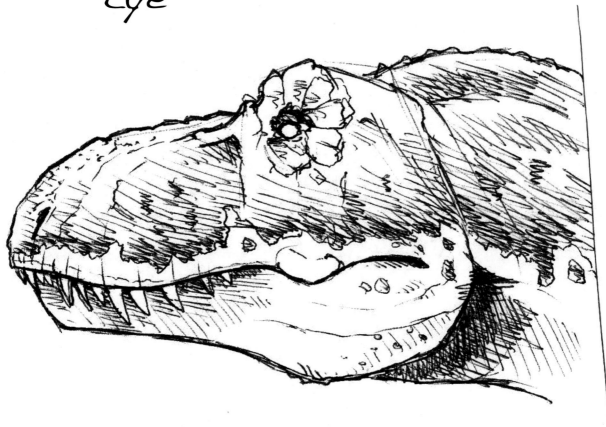

Fun Fact:

Kentrosaurus' tail was unusually long and flexible, and while swinging it back and forth, the tip may have reached 50 miles per hour.

Oviraptor

Oviraptor is a small therapod from Mongolia first discovered in 1924 by famed dinosaur hunter, Roy Chapman Andrews. Its name means "egg stealer" because its fossilized remains were discovered near eggs. However, in 1990, new oviraptorid skeletons were found on top of a nest full of eggs. *Oviraptor* wasn't stealing eggs – it was sitting on them, just like birds do today! Also like modern birds, *Oviraptor* had a toothless beak, specialized hip bones called a pygostyle, and they were even covered in feathers. We still aren't sure what *Oviraptor* ate, but its powerful beak may have helped it to eat a variety of things, like lizards and clams.

Fun Fact:

Henry Fairfield Osborn, who first described and named *Oviraptor*, warned that its name may be misleading, and guessed that the dinosaur may have actually been brooding its eggs. He was right, of course, be we wouldn't know that for at least 70 more years!

Edmontosaurus

Edmontosaurus was one of the biggest hadrosaurs, or duck-billed dinosaurs. They reached 40 feet long and 4 tons and probably were social animals, living in herds across what is now western North America. They must have eaten a lot of plant material every day, and aquatic plants may have been among their favorites. Spending time in the water may have also protected them from predators, like *T. rex*, but swamps and ponds were teeming with predators too, especially crocodiles. Fortunately for these *Edmontosaurs*, *Leidysuchus* was a small crocodile that likely only at fish, small reptiles, and amphibians.

The Artist's Eye

Fun Fact:

Paleontologists have excavated many *Edmontosaurus* skeletons, and as a result, we know a lot about them. Their skulls were more than 3 feet long and fossilized skin impressions have even shown us what their skin looked like.

Giganotosaurus

Just as *Tyrannosaurus rex* was the apex predator of western North America during the Late Cretaceous, *Giganotosaurus* was terrorizing everything in its path in South America. *Giganotosaurus*, which means "giant southern lizard," was nearly as big as *T. rex* at almost 45 feet long, and may have been able to chase down prey up to 31 miles per hour. This fearsome dinosaur wasn't alone, though. *Giganotosaurus* shared its habitat with, and probably often competed with another large therapod, called *Ekrixinatosaurus*. Why so many large theropods in one place? Patagonia during the Late Cretaceous was also home to many titanosaurs!

The Artist's Eye

Majungasaurus
ANSP 07

Fun Fact:

Giganotosaurus belonged to a fearsome group of predators. Together with its closest relatives, they formed a group called the Carcharodontosaurids.

Lesothosaurus

Not all dinosaurs were enormous beasts. Little *Lesothosaurus* was only a few feet long and no taller than a turkey. Named after Lesotho, a tiny country in southern Africa where it was found, this dinosaur was probably a swift herbivore that inhabited the desert ecosystems of the region during the Early Jurassic Period. It had very large eyes, which paleontologists think helped it to see well at night and scan the horizon for the many predators that surely would have made a meal of this small species. Some paleontologists believe *Lesothosaurus* was an early ancestor of nearly all ornithischian dinosaurs.

The Artist's Eye

Fun Fact:

Lesothosaurus had small hands and a peculiar beak, but its many teeth were serrated and designed for shredding vegetation.

Velociraptor

Velociraptor may have been a swift, cunning, dangerous predator, but only to small reptiles, amphibians, and small dinosaurs. That's because despite what you may have seen in movies, *Velociraptor* was not much bigger than a turkey – a very angry turkey. Paleontologists also now know that *Velociraptor* was covered in feathers even though it couldn't fly, and some even think they may have hunted in packs, like wolves and hyaenas. This would have allowed them to take down much bigger prey than they could have alone. These swift, agile predators belonged to the dromaeosaurids, the group of dinosaurs that evolved into modern birds.

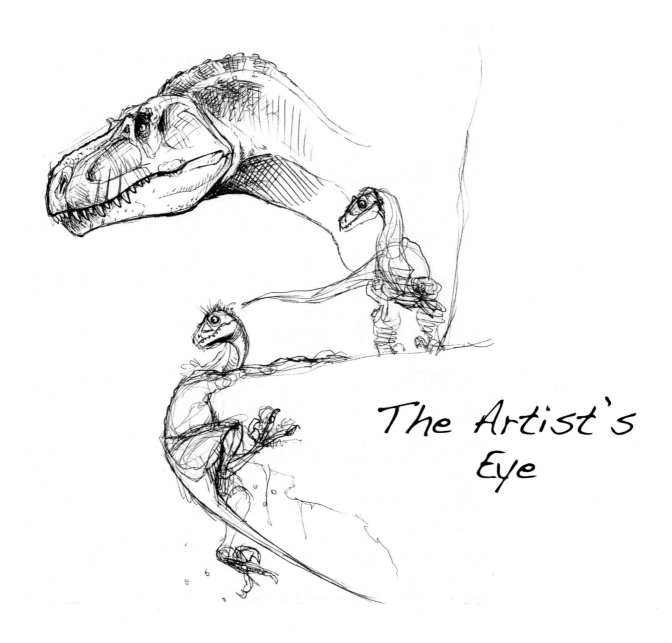

The Artist's
Eye

Fun Fact:

Velociraptor may be more like a turkey than you think. Their skeletons, as with all dromaeosaurids, are almost indistinguishable from the skeletons of modern birds.

Gryposaurus

Gryposaurus, which means hooked-nosed lizard, inhabited western North America during the Late Cretaceous Period. Named for its nasal hump, this herbivorous hadrosaurid dinosaur grew to nearly 30 feet in length. Despite its pronounced nasal hump, *Gryposaurus* was a member of the Hadrosaurines, or the crestless hadrosaurids. Dinosaur skeletons are very rarely found complete, so sometimes it can be very difficult to figure out which dinosaurs are related to each other, or even if a "new' species is actually one already discovered. Paleontologists have long argued over whether *Grypsourus* is actually *Kritosaurus*.

The Artist's Eye

Fun Fact:

Gryposaurus is one of the most geographically wide-ranging dinosaur species known. It has been found from Texas to Alberta, Canada.

Diabloceratops

With its curved frill horns and another horn right above each eye, *Diabloceratops* is certainly one of the most distinctive ceratopsian dinosaurs. It also has a very distinctive name – *Diabloceratops* means "devil horn-face." This dinosaur lived alongside many others, like *Gryposaurus* and *Euoplocephalus*, in western North America during the Cretaceous Period, and may be an ancestor of its more famous relative, *Triceratops*. It is also a new species; described only in 2010. It is exciting to paleontologists that even in heavily explored regions like the American West, there is still much to learn and discover.

Water-Buffalo
ASIA AMNH

The Artist's Eye

Fun Fact:

Dinosaurs are famous for having strange-looking features or body shapes, but many scientists will tell you that the most bizarre animal in the history of life on Earth is the lowly turtle.

Chasmosaurus

At about 16 feet long and weighing 2 tons, *Chasmosaurus* was an average-sized ceratopsian. It lived in the Late Cretaceous Period in western North America, and like other ceratopsians, it had facial horns and a neck frill. What is most distinctive about this ceratopsian, however, are the two large holes in the frill. Paleontologists debate how this dinosaur defended itself. It could not outrun predators, and its modest size didn't deter them either. The horns were so short they would not have been much help, and the large holes in the neck frill make it useless as a shield. So, how did *Chasmosaurus* protect itself and what was that big shield used for?

The Artist's Eye

Zuniceratops

Fun Fact:

During much of the Cretaceous Period, North America was split into two subcontinents by a shallow sea, called the Western Interior Seaway. The western subcontinent was called Laramidia, and in the east there was Appalachia.

Bambiraptor

Bambiraptor is a small therapod – no more than three feet long and weighing less than five pounds – that lived in Laramidia during the Late Cretaceous Period. Its nearly complete skeleton was found by a boy who was hiking with his family in 1993. *Bambiraptor* belongs to the dromaeosaurid dinosaurs – the lineage that lead directly to modern birds. This diminutive dinosaur was covered in feathers and was probably was a swift runner, but some paleontologists believe that it was arboreal, meaning it lived in trees. We also know it was smart – its brain was the biggest of all the dinosaurs compared to its body size.

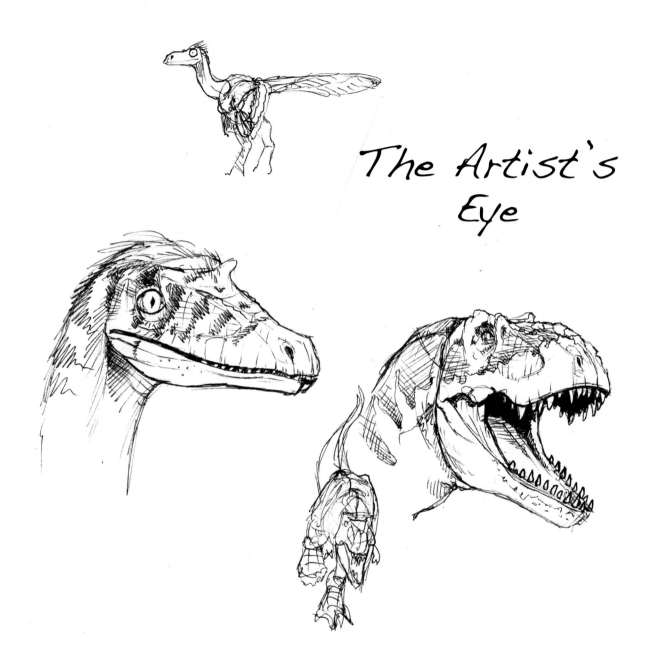

The Artist's Eye

Fun Fact:

Most dinosaurs' names are made up of ancient Latin or Greek words that describe some part of the animal's skeleton, but, it is really up to the paleontologist that discovers the new dinosaur to name it whatever he or she wants. Sometimes they are named after a country, or even a cartoon character, like Bambi.

Allosaurus

Tyrannosaurus rex may have been the king of the dinosaurs in the Late Cretaceous, but *Allosaurus* ruled the land during the late Jurassic Period. This frightening therapod grew to over 30 feet long and is best known from western North America, but it also has been found in Africa and Europe. As the apex predator of its day, *Allosaurus* probably hunted ornithischians like *Stegosaurus*, and if it hunted in packs as some paleontologists believe, it may have even been able to take down the mighty sauropods, like *Brachiosaurus* and *Seismosaurus*. We also know that it grew quickly, especially as a teenager, when it gained over 300 pounds each year.

The Artist's Eye

Baby Allosaurus

Fun Fact:

Dinosaur skeletons that are especially complete and well preserved are often given nicknames by the paleontologists who discover and study them. The most famous *T. rex* specimen is named "Sue," and the most famous *Allosaurus* skeleton is named "Big Al."

Brachiosaurus

Brachiosaurus was an enormous sauropod that lived in the late Jurassic Period in western North America, alongside *Stegosaurus* and *Allosaurus*. Its skull features a pronounced bony ridge above its snout, but its most unusual feature is its long front limbs compared to shorter rear legs. This allowed it to hold its neck up very high to graze on vegetation up to 30 feet above the ground. This specialization was needed because there were several other sauropods living in the same area at that time. The other sauropods were also probably specialized, but for eating lower-growing plants, or even only certain types of plants.

The Artist's Eye

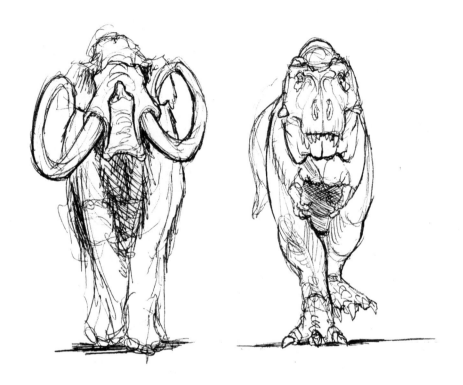

Fun Fact:

The longer front limbs on *Brachiosaurus* is so unusual that paleontologists named it for that feature: *Brachiosaurus* means "arm lizard."

Ceratosaurus

Ceratosaurus was a large predator that lived alongside *Allosaurus* in western North America during the Late Jurassic Period. It was smaller than *Allosaurus*, reaching only 20 feet in length and weighing up to 1 ton. Its name means "horned lizard," referring to the bony, blade-shaped crest on its snout, and the smaller horns, or ridges, over its eyes. Another horned therapod, *Carnotaurus*, was *Allosaurus*' South American relative. Paleontologists believe the nasal horn was probably used for display, or for fighting other *Ceratosaurus* rivals for territory, food, and mates. This dinosaur also had a row of osteoderms, or bony plates, along its back.

Chirp! —

Fun Fact:

Dinosaurs lived a tough life. Their skeletons often reveal signs of healed injuries, broken bones, and even arthritis. Paleopathology is the branch of paleontology that studies these fascinating features and gives us another window into the lives of these long extinct animals.

Camarasaurus and Ceratosaurus

Camarasaurus was a very common sauropod in the Late Jurassic of western North America. It lived alongside other giants, like *Brachiosaurus*, herbivorous dinosaurs like *Stegosaurus*, and among predators like *Allosaurus* and the horned therapod, *Ceratosaurus*. Many therapods had bones that were hollow and rather delicate, so hunting large prey like *Camarasaurus* would have been quite dangerous. Indeed, the skeletons of many therapods often reveal a number of wounds and injuries. That is one reason why paleontologists believe that many predators would have hunted in packs - safety in numbers isn't just for the prey!

Fun Fact:

Have you ever wondered how sauropods could have held up their heads at the end of such long, heavy necks? One way they did it was to lighten that load by having hollow bones. In fact, *Camarasaurus* means "chambered lizard" because its vertebrae are mostly hollow.

Archaeopteryx and Apatosaurus

Believe it or not, *Archaeopteryx*, which was only about the size of a crow, was actually related to *Apatosaurus*, one of the largest animals ever to walk the planet. They were both saurischians. But, was *Archaeopteryx* even a dinosaur? *Archaeopteryx* actually has features of both therapods and modern birds. It is a transitional species between those two groups, and provided some of the earliest evidence for the theory that birds evolved directly from a group of meat-eating dinosaurs. In fact, many paleontologists will tell you that dinosaurs aren't even really extinct. They are flying all around us all the time – we just call them "birds!"

The Artist's Eye

Fun Fact:

Technology has become a much more common tool to paleontologists in recent years. We now commonly use devices to peer inside delicate bones, and even use them to figure out what pigments were used to help color dinosaur skin and feathers when the animals were alive.

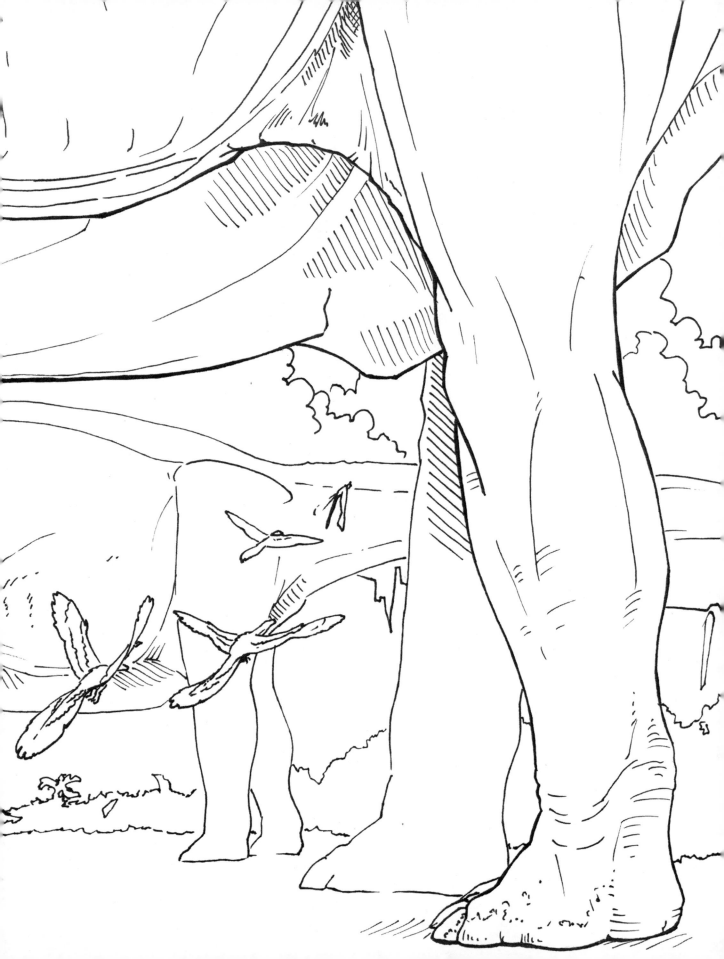

Allosaurus and Seismosaurus

As big as *Allosaurus* was, they probably did not take down prey as big as *Seismosaurus* often. However, as with most predators living today, they probably would not have passed up such a large meal, either. *Seismosaurus*, sometimes also called *Diplodocus*, was truly enormous. It may have grown to be more than 100 feet long and 16 tons. In fact, its name refers to the fact that the ground around it may have shaken with mini earthquakes with every step it took. They were so big that early paleontologists suggested that they must have lived in water, because, it was thought, they must have been too heavy to support their own weight on land.

The Artist's Eye

Fun Fact:

Seismosaurs had a very long, thin, flexible tail. Some paleontologists have speculated that it may have used it as a giant whip, as a defense against attacking predators.

Brachiosaurs

The brachiosaurs were a group of sauropods with front limbs that were longer than their rear limbs. This unusual arrangement, along with their upright necks, made them the tallest dinosaurs, and the tallest animals ever to live on Earth. Other sauropods were longer, but their longer hind limbs prevented them from holding their neck up very high. The brachiosaurs lived mostly during the late Jurassic Period in much of the northern hemisphere. This group is closely related to the titanosaurs, and it included several species, like Brachiosaurus, and the fittingly named *Giraffatitan*.

Fun Fact:

Like *Brachiosaurus*, *Giraffatitan* has a bony arch on its face. Paleontologists aren't sure what this arch was for, but it was probably not for its nostrils, as some early scientists thought.

Tarchia

At almost 30 feet long (9 m) and weighing up to four and a half tons, *Tarchia* is one of the largest ankylosaurid dinosaurs known. Its size and bulk made it a formidable foe to any hungry predators looking for a meal. It inhabited deserts during the Late Cretaceous Period, more than 65 million years ago, in what is now the Gobi Desert of central Asia. How did such a huge herbivore, which must have required a lot of water and large quantities of food each day to thrive in its arid environment? Paleontologists still have a lot more to learn about this dinosaur and its ecosystem. Only with more skeletons and geological studies can we begin to answer questions like these.

The Artist's Eye

Fun Fact:

Tarchia's name means "brainy one" because its skull is so massive.

Edmontonia

With their bulky, squat bodies and armor plating, the Ankylosaurs were the giant armadillos of the dinosaur world. The nodosaurs were a group of ankylosaurs that lacked the infamous tail club, but with their array of body armor and shoulder spikes, they were still a formidable target for even the largest of predators. *Edmontonia* was particularly common in western North America during the Late Cretaceous period. Paleontologists have recovered and studied so many *Edmontonia* skeletons that they recognize at least three species. Each one grew to a length of more than 20 feet (6 m) and weighed several tons.

The Artist's Eye

Fun Fact:

Paleontologists use all kinds of tricks to learn about the ecosystems inhabited by dinosaurs. From tree rings preserved in permineralized ("petrified") wood found near *Edmontonia* skeletons, we know that they experienced pronounced wet and dry seasons.

About the Artist:

Jason Poole hatched in 1970 someplace in the eastern United States where he was raised by squirrels. His interest in art was spawned as he learned to read from discarded comic books and fast food menus in the mean streets of Philadelphia. To this day the dynamic line art of comic books has left an impression on "Mr. Poole" as he is called by his jungle friends.

Mr. Poole has produced art for several museums and for National Geographic and National Geographic World magazines as well as several scientific publications.

Jason enjoys cheese-burgers and long walks in the badlands of Montana and Wyoming and spending time with his offspring and life mate.

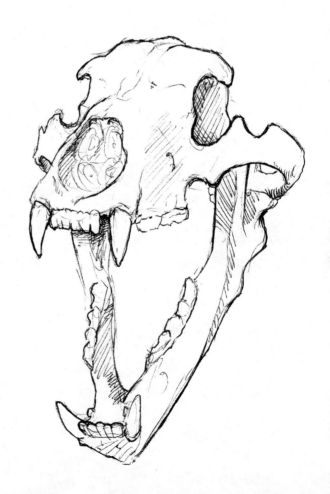

Jason's studio is nestled in East Oak Lane. Its lead lined walls and roof just barely keep out the scans from the mother ship. It's a good life and it is mine.

Cheers, There is some truth in this and that is how it was written in the beginning...

About the Writer:

Jason P. Schein is a writer, naturalist, explorer, and a paleontologist. He has participated in paleontological expeditions in Argentinean Patagonia and across the U.S., and continues to lead expeditions as the head of the Bighorn Basin Dinosaur Project in Montana and Wyoming.

He holds a B.S. and an M.S. in geology from Auburn University, and has taught geology and paleontology at universities in Alabama and Philadelphia, Pennsylvania. He has published numerous papers and abstracts on a wide variety of subjects, including paleoecology, extinct fish, crocodiles and giant turtles, and the end-Cretaceous mass extinction.

Jason is currently the Assistant Curator of Natural History at the New Jersey State Museum. He lives in Philadelphia, PA, where he fills his time by sharing his love of the natural world with his family and by being a dad.